The Best Book of Bikes

Amy Pinchuk

Illustrated by Tina Holdcroft and Allan Moon

MAPLE
TREE
PRESS

Maple Tree Press Inc.

51 Front Street East, Suite 200, Toronto, Ontario M5E 1B3

"Popular Mechanics for Kids" is a trademark of Hearst Communications, Inc.

Text © 2003 by Amy Pinchuk
Illustrations © 2003 by Tina Holdcroft, and © 2003 by Allan Moon

Distributed in the United States by Firefly Books (U.S.) Inc. 230 Fifth Avenue, Suite 1607, New York, NY 10001

We acknowledge the financial support of the Canada Council for the Arts, the Ontario Arts Council, and the Government of Canada through the Book Publishing Industry Development Program (BPIDP) for our publishing activities.

Dedication

Dedicated to my wonderful parents, Phyllis and Abe Pinchuk.

Acknowledgments

Thanks Keltie for graciously wading through such a large pile of manuscript and extracting this book. Thanks Sheba for making this book happen and to Word & Image, Allan, and Tina for making it look great. Thanks to my children Matthew, Rachel, Paul, and Daniel for patiently sitting on all those bikes while I snapped photos, and for being such great kids. Thanks Mark for everything. Thanks David, Lenny, Josh, and my nieces and nephews for all of your help. Thanks to all of my incredible friends for all of your help and support. Thanks to everyone at Martin's Swiss Cycle, Montreal, Quebec, and, Cycle and Sports Paul, Pointe-Claire, Quebec, for all the time and help that you provided. The "Unrideable Bicycle" on page 26 was invented by David E. H. Jones. The Robert Schumann Fast Fact on page 13 is from the Guinness Web site.

Cataloguing in Publication Data

Pinchuk, Amy Ruth, 1959-

The best book of bikes / Amy Ruth Pinchuk; illustrators, Allan Moon and Tina Holdcroft.

(Popular mechanics for kids)

Includes index.

ISBN 1-894379-43-8 (bound)   ISBN 1-894379-44-6 (pbk.)

1. Bicycles—Juvenile literature. I. Moon, Allan II. Holdcroft, Tina III. Title.

TL412.P55 2003   j629.227'2   C2002-904072-8

Design & Art Direction

Word & Image Design Studio
(www.wordandimagedesign.com)

Illustrations

Tina Holdcroft: Page 3 (bottom), 7, 8, 12-13, 15, 18 (top), 21, 23 (top), 25, 26-47, 48 (top), 50 (top), 52 (top left), 54, 55 (top right), 57, 58-59 (main), 60 (middle), 61.

Allan Moon: Page 5, 16-17, 18 (bottom), 19, 20, 22, 23 (bottom), 48 (bottom), 49, 50 (bottom), 51, 52, 53, 55, 59 (top right), 60 (bottom), 62.

Photo Credits

Cover: Scott Markewitz/Getty Images; 3 (top right): courtesy Shane Jenkins/www.bmxultra.com; 3 (middle): Bill Smith/The Wheelmen/www.thewheelmen.org; 4: Duomo/CORBIS/MAGMA; 6 (main): codex atlanticus: f. 133 verso (bicicletta)/Ambrosian Library, Milan; 6 (inset): Ms. B, fol. 83 verso/Réunion des Musées Nationaux/Art Resource, NY; 8 (top): NMPFT/Science & Society Picture Library; 8 (bottom): courtesy The Bicycle Museum of America/New Bremen, OH; 9 (top): Hulton Archive by Getty Images; 9 (bottom): Bill Smith/The Wheelmen/www.thewheelmen.org; 10 (top): courtesy DaimlerChrysler AG; 10 (middle): Sean Sexton Collection/CORBIS/MAGMA; 10 (bottom): Hulton Archive by Getty Images; 11 (top): courtesy The Bicycle Museum of America/New Bremen, OH; 11 (bottom): courtesy LeQuan Brummer/Lightning Cycle Dynamics; 14: courtesy DaimlerChrysler AG; 19: Richard Porath/The Wheelmen/www.thewheelmen.org; 21 (top): Cor Vos; 21 (bottom): EMPICS Sports Photo Agency; 24: Hulton Archive by Getty Images; 29: Phil Schermeister/CORBIS/MAGMA; 32: courtesy LeQuan Brummer/Lightning Cycle Dynamics; 35 (main & inset): courtesy Shane Jenkins/www.bmxultra.com; 36: Charlie Samuels/CORBIS/MAGMA; 38: Tuan Do-Duc; 39: Tuan Do-Duc; 40: Marketa Navratilova/Cor Vos; 41 (top): Frank Fife/AFP; 41 (middle): De Waele/Iso Sport; 42-43 (middle): Richard Hamilton Smith/CORBIS/MAGMA; 43 (inset): Reuters NewMedia Inc./CORBIS/MAGMA; 44: courtesy Vince Marcotte; 46: Reuters NewMedia Inc./CORBIS/MAGMA; 49: courtesy NASA Dryden Flight Research Center; 56: courtesy Toronto Police Service.

Printed in Hong Kong

A   B   C   D   E   F

Contents

Your Ticket to Ride

Pedal power rules! Bikes don't need fuel—just the power of your feet. When it comes to personal transportation, bikes are number one in the world.

What makes bikes such lean, mean machines? Fasten your helmet and zoom in on the popular mechanics of bikes to find out. Ride back in time and check out how bikes were invented. Shift gears to see how bikes work and how they stay up without tipping over as you ride.

Grip your handlebars and steer into the fast and crazy worlds of BMX and racing. Then grab a bike wrench and unwind through the Grease Monkey Zone for expert tips on bike maintenance and repair.

Find out how to gear up for the road before a cross-country trek. And coast through radical stories and cool facts along the way. Enjoy the ride and get the info you need. After all, bikes are number one, especially for having fun.

In a contest of numbers, bikes beat cars hands down. In 2002, there were 340 million cars in the world versus 1.4 billion bikes.

The "Wheel" Thing?

History experts were stunned when they discovered the bike drawing below in a notebook of the Italian inventor Leonardo da Vinci. (Da Vinci was also a great artist who painted the *Mona Lisa*.) The bike looks just like the safety bicycle that was invented in 1885. But the drawing is dated for the year 1490—almost 400 years before the safety bicycle was invented!

So some experts say the sketch wasn't drawn by da Vinci at all. They think a trickster drew it after the bicycle was invented and then slipped it into da Vinci's notebook. Why? To give Italy all the credit for inventing the bike! But others say da Vinci was a great inventor and, if anyone could have sketched the bicycle 400 years before it existed, it was him.

The fact is, da Vinci drew the helicopter sketch below long before the actual machine was ever invented. Look closely at the two sketches. What do you think? Is the bike drawing the "wheel" thing?

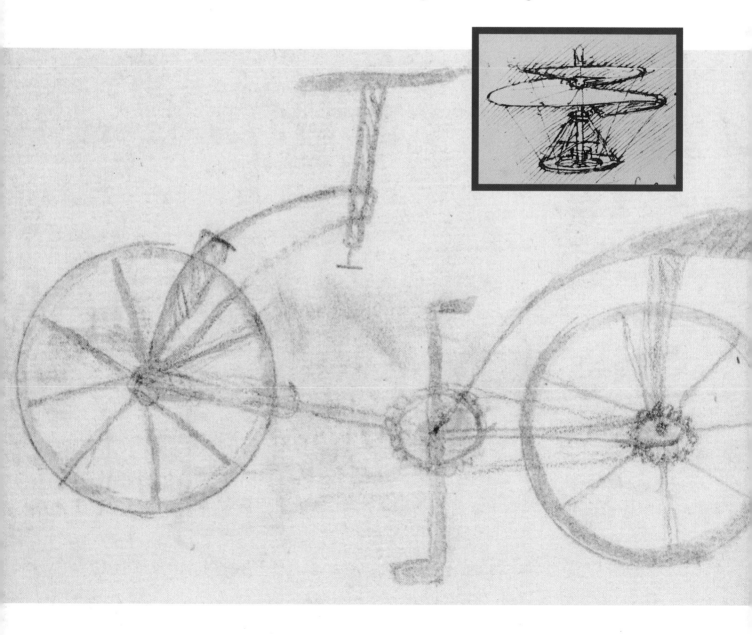

Bikers' World

When it comes to getting around, nothing beats a bike. No other land vehicle can transport people long distances on human power only. What's more, the average kid can run at about 11 km/h (7 mph) but can cycle as fast as 24 km/h (15 mph)! A bike can go so far so fast, because it needs only a small pedal push to move a long way. But it didn't become such a "ticket to ride" overnight. It took inventors hundreds of years to come up with the lean, mean machines we have today. Check out their bright ideas along the way.

Ride Back in Time

3000+ BC   *The first wheel rolls into the world.*

THINGS GET ROLLING

Nobody knows who invented the wheel. It was made more than 5000 years ago around the time when the ancient Egyptian pyramids were built. Archeologists, or people who study ancient remains, think the first wheels were used for making pottery—not transportation!

Around 3000 – 2000 BC, wheels like this one were used for chariots.

1790   *A wooden toy horse becomes the world's first bike.*

Riding the vélocifère was a blast—if you didn't crash!

JUST HORSING AROUND

During the Industrial Revolution in the late 1700s, many mechanical machines and methods were developed to make life easier. And that's when Monsieur de Sivrac of France came up with a brilliant idea for how people could get around more easily. He thought that people could ride a large version of a two-wheeled toy horse! De Sivrac made one out of wood and named his invention the vélocifère from the Latin words for fast (*velox*) and carrier (*ferre*). The vélocifère had two wheels, but no pedals or steering mechanism. People rode it just like a toy horse. They straddled their legs on either side and pushed themselves forward with their feet—hoping not to bump into anything on the way!

1817   *Baron Karl von Drais adds handlebars for steering.*

FATHER OF THE BIKE

The vélocifère was fun to ride, but bikers couldn't steer it. So they often bashed into things until 1817, when Baron Karl von Drais of Germany hit upon an ingenious idea for steering. Von Drais bolted wooden handlebars onto a triangle shape that turned the bike's front wheel. Then riders could steer the bike by turning the handlebars. Von Drais also discovered that by steering zigzag—first one way then the other—bikers could balance the bike and not fall over! For the first time, people could ride on something that could go a long way with just a little push. The new machine went uphill as fast as a person could walk and zoomed across flat land as fast as a galloping horse. So it was called the "swift walker" or "dandy horse" and von Drais was named the "father of the bicycle"!

The swift walker had not only handlebars but armrests for riders to relax and lean on.

FAST-FOOTED PEDALS

Bikers were still pushing their feet along the ground to ride. Something had to be done to get their feet out of the mud. Around 1840, blacksmiths all over the world forged a solution out of metal—pedals and cranks. The pedals fit onto the cranks and the cranks attached directly to the bike's front wheel. Then when bikers pushed the pedals, the cranks turned the front wheel. Finally after 50 years of pushing, the bicycle could be pedaled! It was renamed velocipede, or "fast foot." Each time the pedals turned once around, the front wheel turned once around. That meant the larger the front wheel, the farther the bicycle would go on each pedal turn. So bike inventors began to make front wheels as big as possible and eventually the "high wheeler" was born.

Bikers called the velocipede the "bone shaker" for its rough ride.

HIGH-WHEELING INTO DANGER

High wheelers were a big hit. But if a rider hit a bump or suddenly stopped, the bike cartwheeled and the rider "took a header." In fact, bikers often fell on their heads when they hit the brakes! In 1885, John Kemp Starley of England changed all that when he invented the chain and gear system. In a gear system, pedals and cranks turn a chainring. A chain hooks onto the chainring and a small sprocket, or gear wheel, near the bike's rear wheel. As you pedal, the chainring turns, pulling the chain, which turns the sprocket, which turns the rear wheel. Since the chainring is much larger than the sprocket, one turn of the chainring turns the sprocket many times. This makes the rear wheel go around several times each time the pedals go around once. So bikes no longer needed large front wheels to get the most distance out of a pedal push. Since the new bikes with gear systems and same-size wheels were much more stable than high wheelers, they were called "safety bicycles."

Bikers who rode high wheelers called themselves the fastest men on Earth.

Today, all bikes have a chain and gear system of at least one gear. If your bike is a 3-speed, it has 3 speeds, or gears. If it's a 10-speed, it has 10.

Bike to the Future... ▶

1886   *The first car "putt-putts" around.*

THE CAR IS BORN

Gottlieb Daimler of Germany invented the car by adding a gas motor to a horse-drawn wagon in 1886. He called it a "horseless carriage." But back then it wasn't much competition for bikes, because the car couldn't go as fast as the two-wheeled machines.

Wilhelm Daimler takes his dad, inventor Gottlieb Daimler, for a stroll, er, roll in the world's first car.

1888   *Air-filled tires pump comfort into bike rides.*

Were these adults just kidding around? No way! They were riding this tricycle to get around town.

TRIKES AREN'T JUST FOR KIDS

Until the safety bicycle was invented (see page 9), tricycles were much more stable than bikes. So many adults rode them to and fro. Doctors even rode tricycles for emergency house calls! But in 1888, John Dunlop of Scotland noticed that his son's trike wasn't much fun to ride. Its standard hard, solid tires made the ride bumpy and uncomfortable. So Dunlop replaced them with air-filled tires, which he thought would absorb shocks without jolting the rider. And that's exactly what happened. The air-filled tires made bikes more comfortable and safe to ride. Soon they were pumped up on bikes everywhere, and people all over the globe started biking for work, travel, and fun.

1899   *The invention of the Derailleur gear system lets bikers choose gears, making it easier to pedal up and down hills.*

1903   *Some of the world's first flying machines have built-in bicycles.*

A FLYING BIKE?

Bicycles were the best way to get around in the early 1900s. So some inventors used them in the first airplanes for take-off and landing. But many of their flying machines never got off the ground.

A bike powered this "Cycloplane"—one of inventors' first attempts at a flying machine.

1969 *Humans land on the moon and bikes are built with space-age materials to make them lighter, stronger, and faster.*

1979 *Bikers no longer have to soup up road bikes to go mountain biking.*

A BIKE FOR CLIMBING MOUNTAINS

Bikers head off the road on the world's first official mountain bike—a short, sturdy bike with wide, knobby tires designed for rough and rugged terrain.

Check out the Sidewinder, one of the world's first mountain bikes. It wasn't much more than a standard frame outfitted with fat tires!

2000 *Bike suspension systems spring forward to smooth out all kinds of on- and off-road riding.*

Future *What will bike inventors dream up next?*

BLUE STREAK OF LIGHTNING

Will this strange-looking bike become the most popular long-distance bike of the future? Only time will tell! The Lightning F40's blue cover, called a fairing, helps it slice through air 16 km/h (10 mph) faster than regular bikes. Speed on!

The recumbent bike Lightning F40 cycled the Race Across America in record time at an average speed of 40 km/h (25 mph).

Bikes Rule!

What's the most popular kind of personal transportation in the world? Forget cars, trains, boats, and planes. It's bikes, bikes, and bikes! Check out some fun facts that make bikes rule.

Welcome to Biker Land

More than 75 percent of the people in Germany ride bikes.

Take a Hike, er, Bike

Ride the Trans Canada Trail, which winds through every province and territory in Canada. At over 18 000 km (11 000 mi), it's the world's longest recreational trail for cyclists, hikers, horses, and skiers.

Need for Speed

In 1995, Fred Rompelberg of the Netherlands hit the world's fastest cycling speed just for an instant: 268.8 km/h (167 mph). That's as fast as the average Formula One race car!

21-Day Race

Get set for the Tour de France bicycle race—the world's most popular sports event. Watch cyclist teams pedal more than 3400 km (2125 mi) through the countryside and mountains of France.

Home of the 41-Wheeler

The world's longest "bicycle," a 41-wheel tandem with a 120-m (394-ft) long chain, was built in Italy in 1998 just for the fun of setting the longest bike record. The bike measures a lengthy 25.9 m (84 ft)!

Off the Beaten Track

Believe it or not, over 80 percent of all bikes sold in the U.S. are off-road bikes. It's the birthplace of mountain bikes and off-road cycling!

Tiny Wheelie

The world's smallest rideable bicycle was built in Poland in 1998. Its front wheel is as tiny as a jacket button! So it's definitely not for long treks. The bike's inventor just managed to ride it for 5 m (16 ft) straight.

The Wheel Is Born

The world's first wheel rolled into Mesopotamia—modern-day Iraq—about 5000 years ago.

Bike Cargo Express

It's a cab, it's cargo, it's a bike driven for hire! India has oodles of cargo-carrying and taxi bikes—1 700 000 and counting.

Where Racing Rocks

You can bet on seeing some great bike races in Japan. Keirin Bicycle Racing is bike track racing much like horse racing. People even bet on the winners!

King of the Road

Bicycles rule the road in China. In 2000, there were 450 million bicycles and only 17 million cars.

Bike Parts to Go

Not only does China have the most bikes in the world, it also makes most of the world's bike parts. Maybe it should be called Bike-opolis!

Fast Fact

In 1993, 11-year-old Robert Schumann biked around the world in eight seconds flat! He went to the South Pole with his dad and planted a flag at the pole—the place where all the world's geographic longitude lines meet. Then he biked around the flag, crossing all the lines around the world.

A Motorbike with Training Wheels?!

Want to bet you'll never see one of these in the action movies? Back in 1885, inventor Gottlieb Daimler of Germany wanted to test a new gas-powered engine he had built. So he put it on a safety bicycle that had training wheels.

Lo and behold, the world's first motorcycle was born (see below). However, it took 10 more years of work to develop a safe and well-balanced motorcycle. But that didn't stop Daimler from installing the engine in a car in 1886.

Daimler went on to start the Daimler Motor Company, which became Daimler-Benz, renowned for Mercedes Benz cars. Later he joined forces with the Chrysler car company to found DaimlerChrysler, one of the largest car companies in the world. And to think that it all started with a bike!

Lean Mean
MACHINE

Hop on and ride till you drop! Pump those pedals, shift those gears, and burn some rubber on those two wheels! Whether your bike's a BMX, road, or mountain machine, it's made of cool parts that take you where you want to go. Find out how bikes are built to ride, how to ride a bicycle fit for you, and how the Wright brothers used bicycle parts to build the world's first flying machine.

Made of Cool Parts

What makes a bike such an awesome machine? It's built to ride! Check out its parts and how they work together.

Saddle

Saddle up! Bike saddles come in all shapes and sizes. They're usually made of leather or nylon and some have built-in springs, gels, or foam padding for comfort. They spread your weight evenly to help you balance just like horse saddles do.

Frame

The frame holds you up and keeps the parts of your bike together. It's made of hollow, metal tubes. That way it's light enough for pedaling but strong enough to carry you.

Wheel

Spin your head around wheels on page 20.

Rear wheel sprockets

Derailleur

It de-rails and re-rails the chain. See page 22.

Seat tube

Chain and Chainrings

You may ride your bike, but the chain drives it! The chain is made of steel links that loop onto teeth on the chainrings and rear wheel sprockets. As you push the pedals, the chainring turns, pulling the chain. This turns the rear wheel sprocket, which turns the rear wheel, which propels the bike forward.

Height

The height of a bike is the distance from the top of the seat tube to the ground. Tall bikes are good for speed, because they allow for large wheels, which go farther than small ones on each pedal push. But short bikes like BMX models are good for stability, because they keep riders closer to the ground. What height is right for you? See page 18.

Crank

The pedals are attached to arms called cranks. As you push the pedals, the cranks turn the chainring.

What do bike frames have in common with the Golden Gate Bridge in San Francisco? They're both made of triangles for strength. Triangles spread weight evenly over all three sides, which helps resist bending and twisting under heavy loads.

Hot Handlebars

Curved drop handlebars

help racers hold a crouched position to cut wind drag that slows them down.

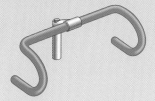

Straight handlebars

are perfect for mountain bikes. They give riders a comfortable upright position along with a good grip and extra control.

Road racing handlebars

allow racers to relax their arms and stretch their backs during marathon races.

BMX handlebars

have a cross-brace for extra strength for racing and aerial tricks.

Handlebars

The handlebars allow you to turn the front wheel, so you can steer the bike. They also help position your body in a good posture for riding. And they just look cool (see right)!

Gear shifter

Get behind these controls on page 23.

Cable

Cables communicate your commands. See page 23.

Brake

Check out how brakes work on page 22.

Front fork

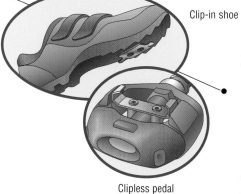

Clip-in shoe

Clipless pedal

Pedals

Pedals are made to be pushed around by your feet. No joke! Everyday riding pedals are flat with metal teeth, or rubber bumps, to give your feet good grip. Some high-performance pedals made only for racers and expert riders lock onto the bottom of special cycling shoes (see left). That way riders' feet can push them down and then pull them up quickly without sliding off.

Check It Out

BICYCLE FIT FOR YOU

If the bike fits, ride it! A bike that fits you properly ensures that your entire leg muscles are used to pedal and that your riding position is correct. A bike that doesn't fit well can lead to uncomfortable, unstable, and inefficient riding. So here are some basic points to help you fit your bike right.

FRAME SIZE

Hop on the bike and stand with both feet flat on the ground. If it's a mountain bike, you should have 2.5 cm (1 in) of clearance between your body and the top tube of the frame (see right). This gives you maneuverability and protection in rough terrain. If it's a road bike, you should have 1 to 2 cm ($\frac{3}{8} - \frac{6}{8}$ in) of clearance.

SADDLE HEIGHT

Sit on the saddle and put one foot on a pedal at the bottom of the pedaling stroke (see left). Now check how much your knee is bent. It should bend only very slightly, so your entire leg muscle is used for pedaling. If it's too bent (far left) raise the saddle so it's "perfectly bent" (center). Or if it's too straight (near left), lower the saddle.

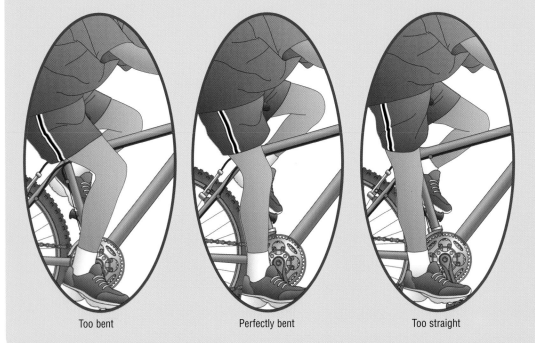

Too bent   Perfectly bent   Too straight

HANDLEBAR HEIGHT

If it's a road bike, you'll want to ride in a crouched, aerodynamic position. Adjust the the handlebar post so the handlebars are 2.5 to 7.5 cm (1 – 3 in) lower than the saddle. You may have to try several positions to find the height that's most comfortable for you. If it's a mountain bike, adjust the handlebars so they are about 2.5 cm (1 in) lower than the saddle (see right).

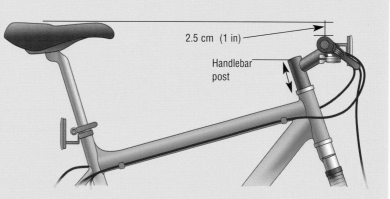

2.5 cm (1 in)

Handlebar post

Handlebar stem

Hub

HANDLEBAR STEM

Many mountain and road bikes have an adjustable handlebar stem (see left). Once everything else is fitted, sit on your bike as if you're ready to ride and look down at the front wheel hub. When the handlebar stem is the proper length, the center bar of the handlebars should just block the hub from view. Adjust it as necessary.

Biker Girls

Back in the 1800s, bikes were a real breakthrough for women. Suddenly, women had a vehicle that they could use by themselves to get around and go places. In fact, until the 1980s, bikes were built for girls with a slanted top tube, so girls could ride in skirts without being "unladylike"—lifting a leg up high to get on and off. But nowadays, kids' bike frames are designed and built basically the same way for girls and boys.

The Wheels

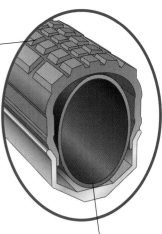

Tread

The tire tread is thick and hard to protect the inner tube from sharp, rough objects on the road. Smooth treads are great for indoor tracks, but can't grip wet roads or grass. Thick, knobby treads with deep furrows give BMX and mountain bikers a great grip on mud, snow, and sand.

Inner tube

The inner tube is like a balloon. It holds air in the tire without bursting or leaking. When you get a flat, the inner tube loses air. Something has pierced it or air is leaking out through the air valve.

W hy are spokes so skinny and what are those weird racing wheels you see on TV? Get the inside scoop on bike wheels.

Tire

Bike tires have two parts: an outer tread and an inner tube.

Air valve

The air valve is used to inflate the inner tube with air.

Hub

This is the center part of the wheel where spokes attach.

Rim

The rim holds the tire and spokes in place.

Spokes

Most bike wheels can hold the weight of an average 11-year-old... plus that of two gorillas! The skinny spokes give the wheels strength without adding the weight of a solid disk wheel. The spokes are set in a pattern that spreads their strength evenly around the wheel.

Nipples

The spokes are mounted on the wheel by screwing them into the nipples. This stretches the spokes between the hub and the rim just like strong elastic bands.

Recommended pressure

You'll find this written on most tires. Tires with high-pressure go fast on smooth surfaces. While those with low-pressure squish over bumps to absorb shocks.

Built Solid for Speed

Racers don't like wheels with spokes. As bikes slice through air at fast speeds, air gets trapped in the spokes. This slows bikes down. So racers prefer lightweight, solid disk wheels that don't let air in. But if wind blows on these wheels from the side, the disks act like sails. The whole bike scoots sideways! Since the front wheel can catch the wind during turns, disks are usually used only on the back wheel during indoor races.

Half and Half

Three-spoke racing wheels are more aerodynamic than regular spoked wheels, because they have fewer spokes to trap air. What's more, even though their spokes are wide, they don't sail like disk wheels. That's because they have big gaps for air to pass through. So three-spoke wheels are often used for outside races and marathons.

Wheeling Your Weight Around

Just how do thin bike wheels wheel your weight around? The spokes and rim are designed to provide strength when the bike is upright and your weight is balanced. When you sit on your bike, the force of your weight pushes down on the wheel hub. This makes the wheel rim flatten out slightly at the bottom and bulge out everywhere else. But the wheel doesn't collapse, because the spokes stretch out and compress just like strong elastic bands. As your weight presses down on the hub, the spokes below the hub compress and the spokes above it stretch out. This allows the spokes to remain straight and the wheel to support your weight. Now that's heavy stuff!

Spoked wheels rolled on the scene about 1000 years after the wheel was invented. People cut out bits of wheels to make them lighter.

The Controls

H ere's the lowdown on how gears and brakes make your bike stop and go.

Wheel rim brake

Wheel rim brakes are the most popular bike brakes around. They're made of two brake pads, one on each side of the wheel rim. When you squeeze the brake lever, the brake pads press on the rim to stop the wheel from turning. And this brings your bike to a stop.

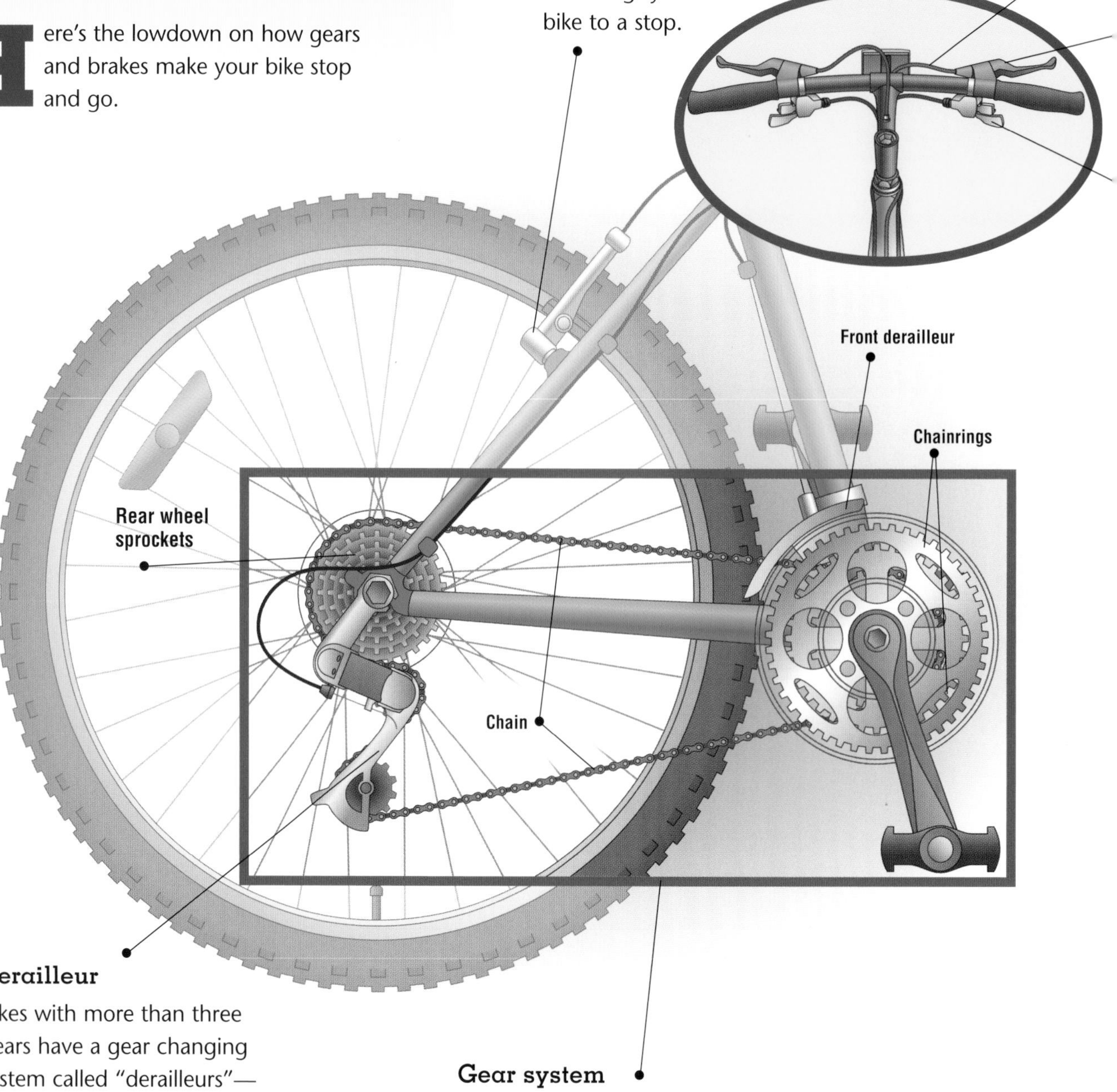

Front derailleur

Chainrings

Rear wheel sprockets

Chain

Derailleur

Bikes with more than three gears have a gear changing system called "derailleurs"— the French word for "taking something off line." And that's exactly what bike derailleurs do when you shift gears. They move the chain onto the chainring and/or rear wheel sprocket for the selected gear.

Gear system

A bicycle has a simple gear system—chainrings, rear wheel sprockets, and chain. It controls how far the bike moves with each pedal push. In the lowest gear (see above right), the bike moves the least distance with each pedal push. In the highest gear (see right), the bike moves the farthest.

Cable

Cables carry your commands to the brakes and gears. For example, when you squeeze a brake lever, it pulls a hidden wire inside the cable that is attached to the brake pads. This moves the pads into action.

Brake lever

Bikes usually have a brake lever on each handlebar. If your bike has a brake on the back wheel only, then both levers control it. But if it has brakes on both wheels, each lever controls a different brake. To find out which lever controls which, see *Check It Out* at the right.

Gear shifter

This lever allows you to change gears. It signals the derailleurs to move the chain into place for the chosen gear:

Lowest gear

The chain moves onto the smallest chainring and the largest rear sprocket.

Highest gear

The chain moves onto the largest chainring and the smallest rear sprocket. All other gears lie between these two extremes.

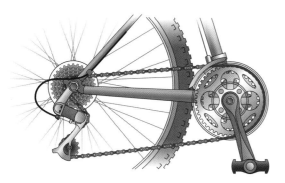

Check It Out

WHICH BRAKE IS WHICH?

Does your bike have front and back brakes? If so, it's important to know which brake lever controls which, because each one affects your bike differently. For example, if you stop quickly with the back brake, your bike may fishtail from side to side. Or if you brake quickly with the front brake, your bike may flip over in a cartwheel. So use both brakes to stop and don't try to stop quickly when you're going fast. To tell which brake is which, squeeze the brake levers, one at a time, and check which brake pads move. To get a feel for how each brake works, ride your bike at the speed of a quick walk and try stopping with each brake.

If you don't have wheel rim brakes and you pedal backwards to brake, you have a coaster brake inside the wheel hub.

From Bicycles to Flying Machines

It's a bike, it's a kite…it's an airplane! Wilbur and Orville Wright, the brothers who invented the world's first engine-powered flying machine, loved tinkering with toys and machines. In 1893, the pair started up the Wright Cycle Company to sell and repair bikes in Dayton, Ohio. And soon after, they became obsessed with building a machine that could fly (see below).

The Wright brothers began making one-person "kites" and powered airplanes. But they needed lots of wind, open space, and a soft landing spot to test them. So for two years, Wilbur and Orville traveled back and forth to a sand dune in Kitty Hawk, North Carolina, to try out their machines.

The traveling took lots of time and money. So the Wright brothers invented a wind tunnel and other machines out of bicycle parts—wheels, gears, and pedals—to test the aircraft in their bike shop before they hit the open air. These testing machines helped them perfect wing shapes and other key parts of the airplane.

In 1903, the Wright brothers returned to Kitty Hawk to try out a new flying machine. And this one worked! Orville flew 36.5 m (120 ft) and stayed in the air for 12 seconds, opening up the skies to human flight.

Zoom In

ON THE MECHANICS

OK, maybe there was never any doubt in your mind that your bike is one radical machine. After all, you're the lucky kid who gets to ride it every single day. And maybe you know exactly what makes its wheels go round— pedal power from your very own two feet! But do you know what helps your bike stay up when you take it for a spin? Or what gear to use when and why? Or just why it is that once you learn to ride a bike you never forget? Zoom in on bike mechanics to find out.

How Bikes Stay Up

If you got off your bike and let it go, it would fall over, right? So what makes it stay up when you ride it? Check out the three things at work.

The "Unrideable" Bicycle

In 1970, a scientist revealed one of the things that helps a moving bike stay up. He built a bicycle that always fell over no matter what the rider did! And it wasn't easy. It took him four tries to get it just right. But his unrideable bicycle showed that the steering mechanism of normal bikes—the handlebars, front forks, and wheel hub—helps keep bikes stable when they're on the move.

The angle of the front forks and the height of the wheel hub help bikes balance naturally and steer themselves to stop from falling over. For example, if you push a bike without a rider, the bike will begin to fall over. As it falls, the front wheel will turn to try to regain its balance. But if the front forks were made at a different angle, as in the unrideable bicycle, this natural balancing act wouldn't happen. The bike would fall over immediately. Kerplunk!

Zigzag Steering

Your steering skill is the second thing that helps a bike stay up as you ride. Remember your very first bike ride? Chances are it was quite wobbly. But once you got the hang of it, you began steering in a series of big zigzags, which helped keep the bike stable. Each time the bike was about to fall over, you turned the front wheel to correct its balance.

At first, it's too tough to steer this way fast enough to stop the bike from tumbling. So you may have wiped out on your first few rides. But with practice your zigzag turns became smaller, because you learned to straighten out the bike before it got too much out of balance. And eventually, you got so good at zigzag steering that now you don't notice it at all!

Frisbee® Physics

The third thing that helps bikes stay up is related to the motion of a Frisbee®. No kidding! When you toss a Frisbee® with spin, it makes a pocket of air and flies on it. The Frisbee® keeps moving and spinning through the air without tilting. That's because once an object is moving and spinning, it tries to keep moving and spinning without changing direction.

The faster the Frisbee® spins, the more it keeps moving in the same direction and the less it wobbles. The same is true of a bicycle. The faster the wheels spin, the more they try to keep moving and spinning in the same direction. And the more the bike is forced to stay up, because any falling or tilting of the wheels will change the direction of moving and spinning. That's why it's easier to balance a bike when it's moving quickly rather than slowly as you first begin to pedal.

Check It Out

READY, STEADY STEERING

Whether you're riding circles around a friend or bombing straight down a hill, you're steering so your bike doesn't fall over. How much steering do you do? Try this experiment and see. Find a smooth, dry path to ride on. Wet your front tire by driving through a puddle or sponging it with water. Now ride your bike in a *straight* line. Then get off your bike and check out the water track it made on the path. See how the track zigzags? It shows how you are constantly steering your bike "back on track."

If steering is so important, how do stunt cyclists ride with no hands? They steer by shifting their body weight instead of the handlebars.

Gear Garage

What do gears do?

Gears help you get the most out of each pedal push. They can help you travel as far or as little as possible each time the pedals turn once around. Each gear has a different gear ratio—the number of times it turns the rear wheel for each pedal turn.

Want to figure out the gear ratio of the gear you're in?

Check which chainring and rear wheel sprocket the chain is on. Count the number of teeth on that chainring and do the same with the sprocket. Then divide the number of chainring teeth by the number of rear sprocket teeth (see right).

3rd Gear

chainring 42 teeth

sprocket 21 teeth

Gear ratio $42 \div 21 = 2$

Why do some bikes have more than one gear?

A variety of gears allows you to pedal at a steady rate, or cadence, as you ride through different terrain. For example, say you're pedaling 60 full pedal rotations, or strokes, per minute on flat ground. Then you start going up a steep hill. Since pedaling uphill is more difficult, it takes more time to complete each stroke. So you can't pedal as many strokes per minute. But if you change to a lower gear when you begin climbing the hill, the chain moves onto a larger rear sprocket. Then the bike moves a smaller distance for each stroke, so it's easier to pedal. And you can keep pedaling at the same cadence.

Going up? Ski hill chair lifts or cable cars run on gear mechanisms that are several kilometres (miles) long. At each end, the lift or car cable loops around large sprocket wheels. These sprockets turn to pull the cable and passengers or cars from one end to the other.

In this gear the rear wheel turns twice for each pedal turn.

How can you tell how many gears a bike has?

The number of "gears," or speeds, is the number of all possible chainring and sprocket combinations. So if you multiply the number of chainrings by the number of rear sprockets, you'll get the number of gears. For example, a mountain bike may have three chainrings and seven sprockets—3 x 7 = 21—for a total of 21 gears. Cool!

Why do you have to pedal when changing gears?

When you're pedaling, the chain is constantly moving, looping on and off the chainring and sprocket teeth. So the derailleurs can easily redirect it to a new sprocket or chainring to change gears. But when you're coasting, the chain isn't moving. So the derailleurs can't get it off the teeth to redirect it.

Fast Fact

Since a bike with "no gears" has one chainring and one rear sprocket, it actually has one gear.

Check It Out

GET IN GEAR

What's your best gear? It all depends on the terrain you're riding in. To get a real feel for the different gears on your bike, try this experiment.

Gear #	Sprocket	Chainring	Start-up	Flat ride feel	Hill ride feel	Comments
1 (low)	S3	C1	Weird	Slow	Easier	Good for hills
2 (medium)	S2	C1	OK	OK	OK	OK
3 (high)	S1	C1	Hard	Fast	Hard	Good for racing

YOU WILL NEED:

- your bike
- washable marker
- paper
- pencil

1 Use the marker to number each rear sprocket on your bike, from smallest to largest. Start with S1 for the smallest (S for sprocket), S2 for the next smallest and so on.

2 Likewise, number the front chainrings, from smallest to largest, starting with C1 for the smallest (C for chainring).

3 On a piece of paper, draw a table like the one above.

4 Ride your bike and shift into first gear. Stop. Then start riding again. How does it feel to start up your bike in this gear? Ride around a bit and notice how it feels. Try riding on flat ground and then up a steep hill—without shifting gears. Get off your bike and see which chainring and sprocket the chain is on. Record your observations in your chart.

5 Repeat step 4 for each gear.

6 Check out the results on your table. Which gears are good for pedaling up hills? Which gears are good for riding fast on flat ground? Riding slow? Keep this table to help get the most out of your bike.

Bikers Never Forget

What do cyclists have in common with elephants? They never forget—how to ride a bike, that is. Once you learn to steer and balance a bike, it becomes as natural as walking. Experts say the human brain can quickly learn simple motor skills, such as cycling, walking, and throwing.

Unlike many non-motor skills, such as remembering phone numbers and addresses, the brain retains learned motor skills even if they aren't used for a long time. So even though your unused cycling skills may get a bit rusty, you'll always remember enough to ride a bike without it falling over.

No Couch Potato

Don't be fooled by the recumbents. They may look like wacky lawn chairs on wheels (see below), but recumbent bikes are designed to be much faster and more energy-efficient than everyday bikes and even racing bikes.

According to official bike racing rules, recumbents are not allowed in most competitions. They give racers an unfair advantage. Their special design cuts down on wind resistance because there are fewer surfaces directly exposed to the wind. Also, the seat of recumbents is built close to the ground for extra stability and control. And the back of the seat provides support that cyclists can push against for extra pedaling power—not to mention comfort!

The fastest flat road speed record for a human powered vehicle is 110.6 km/h (68.7 mph). It was set in 1992 by a recumbent named Cheetah.

BMX AND Racing

Take a deep breath. Hang on tight and pedal your way into the freewheeling worlds of BMX and bike racing. Discover how BMX got off the ground, sick tricks, and the fine art of crashing and burning in the dirt. Meet a champion bike racer and check out how racers bank on speed. Scale a cliff, leap a log, blast through a puddle, and find out what it takes to downhill mountain race. Get into the draft for the inside track on how team spirit rules the race.

BMX Racing

et the inside scoop on the rad and crazy world of BMX racing.

Born of Boredom

What inspired kids to invent BMX racing? Pure boredom—no joke! In the early 1970s, kids of motocross racers often hung around the track as their parents revved motorcycle engines and raced all day long. One day when a few kids got bored (after all they couldn't join in the motocross fun), they invented something cool to do on their bikes—BMX racing. In fact, B is for bike, M is for motor, and X is for cross.

Motocross Without a Motor

BMX is a pedal power version of motocross racing. Bikers race around a short indoor or outdoor dirt track made of whoop-de-doos (see *Talking 'Bout BMX,* right), ditches, berms, jumps, steep curved descents, and obstacles galore. Races are divided according to riders' ages and levels of experience from beginner to expert. Each moto is a timed race of one or many laps around the track. Eight riders start side-by-side. Then they crash and burn as they vie for position at the front of the inside track—the shortest route to the finish line.

Gonzo Gear

BMX racers wear "leathers" that look like motorcycle pants and full-body protective gear— mouth, chest, elbow, knee, and butt guards. But they don't suit up for fashion. Protection is a must for ripping around the track as is a mean BMX machine. In fact, BMX bikes are designed for easy maneuvering, strength, stability, and crashing. They have small wheels and sturdy frames that make it easy for riders to jump and put a foot down during tight turns. They also have thick, knobby tires for gripping mud and bike pads to protect riders when they bang against the bike during landings and crashes. Thrash on!

Talking 'Bout BMX

BMX riders speak a language all their own. Check out some of their words and expressions.

Words to crash by:
crash and burn, wipeout, zonk, dead sailor

Words to compliment a nice stunt or riding hard:
rad, phat, sick, hammer, gonzo, boned out

Words to ride by:
thrashing BMX riding just for fun
taking air going airborne
freestyle or **styling** doing tricks and stunts with a BMX bike
moto BMX race or heat
scuffing using your feet on the tires to brake

Words for stunts, jumps, and obstacles:
whoop big dirt bump race obstacle
whoop-de-doos a bunch of whoops one after the other
berm dirt bank on a turn
bunny hop sequence of small jumps
table top a jump with a flat top. Also, laying the bike sideways in midjump

Some early BMX bikes had motorcycle handlebars.

BMX Freestyle

Buckle up your skid lid (helmet) and follow these tips to get your freestyle career in gear.

1. Make sure it's cool with the folks at home before you start doing tricks.

2. Learn one trick at a time with an expert and practice, practice, practice…

3. Start with simple tricks on the ground before attempting halfpipe (U-shaped ramp) or other ramp tricks.

4. Imagine yourself doing each step of a trick in your mind before you do the trick.

5. When learning a new trick, get some friends to hold your bike and slowly move you through each step.

6. Don't let anybody pressure you to try anything you're not ready for yet.

7. Practice on smooth and hard paved surfaces. Make sure there is no garbage, glass, or rocks around.

8. Never pull tricks or practice in traffic or near blind curves that cars may come around.

9. Crashing is part of learning. Always wear full-body protective gear. Put pads on the bike to protect your body from the frame.

10. Crash the bike—not yourself. Try to bail out and ditch your bike before you crash.

BMX Takes Off

Back in 1976 BMX wasn't enough of a thrill for Bob Haro, a teenage skateboarder who wanted to get airborne on his bike. But using his skateboarding skills, Bob soon had his BMX bike flying off jumps and halfpipes and twirling through the air. He was thrilled! BMX freestyle was born and bike stunts became all the rage. Sport magazines and later popular movies such as *E.T.* featured Bob and his freestyle team taking air. Riders everywhere invented all types of BMX freestyle tricks, such as wheelies, endos, aerials, pop outs, and balancing on just about any part of a moving or stationary bike. Today sick stunts like these are performed by teams and individual riders in freestyle competitions and demonstrations. Riders get top points not only for the execution of tricks but also for creating rad and original tricks.

Sick Tricks

Check out some tricks that give freestyle BMX its kicks:

wheelie riding on the back wheel with the front tire in the air

endo a reverse wheelie with the back tire in the air

can can swinging a leg over the top tube so both legs are on the same side of the bike

pogo moving forward by bouncing the bike, usually on the back tire

pop out riding off the top of the ramp, touching down on the top, spinning around and riding down

aerial a 180-degree turn in midair off the top of a ramp

180, 360, 540, 720, 900 degrees that rider and bike spin around in the air

bar spin spinning the handlebars around completely

tailwhip whipping the back end of the bike around the handlebars in midair while the rider remains forward

superman jumping with the feet straight behind the rider while the rider pushes the bike forward with extended arms

truck driver a 360 with a 360 bar spin

bus driver a truck driver with one hand on the handlebars

pinky squeaks multiple tailwhips while scuffing the tire

E.T. pedaling in midair just like in the movie *E.T.*

nothing jumping with hands and feet off the bike in midair

Meet a Bike Racer

Pro bike racer Paulo Saldanha loves to race because it's fast and aggressive. Paulo's also an exercise physiologist who studies how the human body works. He's interested in how the body reacts to extreme stress. As if competing in the Ironman Triathlon (see *Bio Snapshot* far right) wasn't enough to find out, Paulo entered the Race Across America to really push his body to the limit.

This 5000-km (3108-mi) race coast to coast across the U.S. is the longest and most grueling bike race in the world. Unlike most races, it's non-stop. Apart from brief catnaps, racers cycle day and night until they reach the finish line! Paulo averaged about 20 to 30 km/h (12 – 19 mph) throughout the race. And he rode with special equipment hooked up to his body and bike that monitored his energy intake and output, power output, heart rate, body fat, and hours of sleep.

Sleeping only about 90 minutes every 24 hours, Paulo finished the race in 10 days. He became the first Canadian to ever finish. He also won Rookie of the Year! It took months to recover from the sleep loss and muscle strain, but it was worth it. Paulo learned how to train cyclists to deal with extreme stress and keep going no matter what.

A Close Shave

Many racers shave their legs before a big race. While some racers swear by shaving their legs to make them more aerodynamic, in fact those skinny hairs really don't slow them down. Here's why the pros do it. First, falling is a fact of every bike racer's life, and falls can lead to nasty cuts and scrapes. Some racers call the large scrapes they get "pizza" or "road rash." Hairy legs can trap dirt in the scabs that form over scrapes, which can lead to nasty infections. Yuck! Second, along with lots of training, the pros have deep tissue massages to get into top physical condition. A masseur presses really hard into the racer's leg muscles, and this is tough to do on hairy legs. What's more, if the masseur accidentally pulls leg hairs, it hurts. Ouch! Third, for some racers, shaving their legs puts them in the right mindset for the race.

Bio Snapshot

TWO-TIME CHAMP

Paulo is a two-time Canadian Champion Masters Bike Racer, including both a time trial—race against the clock—and a road race.

IRONMAN RECORD-SETTER

Paulo holds the Canadian record for finishing Hawaii's Ironman Triathlon, a race made up of a 3.9-km (2.4-mi) swim, 180-km (112-mi) bike race, and 42-km (26-mi) run, with the fastest time.

TRAINING MANIAC

Keeping fit for these races is no easy job. Paulo says he did weight training, swam 20 km (12 mi) per week, cycled 500 to 800 km (310 – 497 mi) per week, and ran 70 to 100 km (44 – 62 mi) per week. Whew!

Champion racer Paulo Saldanha cycled the Race Across America in 10 days straight and could still stand up to celebrate.

Get into the Draft

Bike racing is all about putting as much energy as possible into going as fast as possible. Check out how air resistance is a racer's biggest enemy and drafting the weapon used to conquer it.

Hitting a Wall

No cyclist can avoid air. It's everywhere! As racers hit speeds around 30 km/h (19 mph), cycling into air becomes like hitting a wall. The air slows them down, and they have to bike harder to keep up their speed. This air resistance feels like the strong force you feel pushing against your body as you walk headfirst into a strong wind.

Follow the Leader

Racers use drafting to cut down air resistance. They try to line up directly behind a cyclist who's riding out in front, cycling as close as possible without colliding. The idea behind drafting is that the leader uses extra energy to break a hole through the "wall of air." Then the followers can go through the hole without using as much energy. Drafting can save as much as 30 percent of a racer's energy!

Leader of the Pack

Eventually, the leader may get so tired from fighting air resistance that other racers pass her and take the lead. So drafting can lead to amazing group dynamics, or motion, during a race!

Get with the Team Plan

When teams race, it is all for one and one for all. Team races usually have many teams competing against each other with about eight racers per team. Each team chooses a leader—usually the rider who's fastest at climbing hills or riding flats—whatever is most important for the race. The other team riders try to lead the leader through most of the race. That way the leader can ride in their draft to save energy. Then, when the time is right for a strategic sprint, the leader tries to break away into first place and win the race for the team.

The Lone Racer

In individual racing, everyone is out for themselves. So drafting becomes very interesting, because racers have to draft with their opponents! Competing cyclists take turns in the lead. That way they can save energy by drafting for part of the race. Then they pick their moment to try to sprint into first place and win. But it's always hard to catch up from behind. So remember this: hanging out and enjoying the draft too long can leave you in the cold and cause you to lose the race.

Birdbrains Draft Too

Though you won't see geese racing bikes anytime soon, they do save energy by drafting. Zoologists have discovered that geese save up to 27 percent of their energy by flying in V formations. Like bike racers, geese fly one behind another as close as possible without colliding. The stronger geese lead the flock, working the hardest to cut through the air. The weaker and young birds fly at the back to draft with the flock. Research shows that the birds' places in the V shape and the V's angles coincide exactly with those that save the most energy. In fact, saving energy by drafting helps geese migrate long distances. It's the brainy way to fly!

Drafting is part of road racing and marathons. But it's not allowed in time trials or mountain bike or BMX racing, because these races depend solely on riders' athletic ability.

Banking on Speed

What do racers do when they ride around a velodrome—an arena with a gradually banked track? Bank on speed. No kidding! Here's how velodromes help racers cycle at high speeds.

Where Speed Rules

Believe it or not, you can't bike slowly at a velodrome—or else you and your bike will fall over! That's because the outer track is banked, or sloped, at a steep angle designed for bikes traveling at about 80 km/h (50 mph). The banking makes it easier and safer for racers to cycle faster than on a flat track.

Drat—A Flat Track!

On a flat oval track, it takes lots of energy just to hold a bike on course. Racers must steer strongly to provide centripetal force, which keeps objects moving in a circular path. They must also pedal hard as the tires rub against the track to grip it with friction. And the faster a bike goes, the greater the centripetal force and the racer's energy needed to keep on course. The fact is, racers would rather put all this energy into speeding ahead.

"C" Force

And that's exactly what banked tracks let racers do. The banking angle is designed so the track pushes against the bikes. This provides the centripetal force to keep the bikes moving in a circular path, which keeps the speeding racers on the track. Then racers can put more energy into propelling the bikes forward and gaining speed. In fact, the steeper the banking angle, the greater the centripetal force and the faster the speed of the track.

Feel the Force

You can feel centripetal force in action when you whirl an object on a string above your head. As the object goes round, you feel a strain in your arm, which provides the centripetal force to keep it moving in a circle around your head. The faster you twirl the object, the greater the strain you feel and the greater the force. And if you suddenly stop providing the force by letting go of the string, the object will fly through the air in a straight line. (How's that for going off track?)

When the Banking Gets Tough...

Track racers are lucky because the banking angle works in their favor, providing the centripetal force necessary to keep them on track. But BMX and mountain bike racers aren't so lucky. To make races more challenging, many of their trails are banked in the opposite direction, called off-camber banking. So BMX and mountain bike racers have to work extra hard to stay on track!

Velodrome Bike Races

Cyclists meet at the velodrome to compete in the following races:

VELODROME (TRACK) TIME TRIAL: Individual cyclists race against the clock for 500 or 1000 m (547 or 1094 yd). These races hit the fastest speeds, up to 80 km/h (50 mph).

VELODROME SPRINT RACING: Two to four competitors vie for position over 1000 m (1094 yd) and then race to the finish line.

VELODROME INDIVIDUAL PURSUIT: Two riders start at opposite sides of the velodrome and try to catch each other or be first to complete the distance of 2 to 4 km (1.2 – 2.5 mi).

Downhill Mountain Racing

According to mountain bike racer Fred Belanger, also known as "Downhill Fred," "Biking is great fun but you gotta try downhill racing to really feel the thrill!" And he should know. Downhill Fred (see above) has raced all over the U.S. and even competed in the Mammoth Kamikaze—one of the toughest and steepest downhill mountain races around.

So what does it take to race down mountains? Speed, technical riding skills, body conditioning, and guts. Racers ride individually and the fastest time wins. The racecourse starts at the top of a mountain and follows a 1 to 5 km (0.6 – 3 mi) long track that plunges down a steep incline. Look out below!

Downhill racecourses are designed to be as tough as possible. Sharp turns lie at the bottom of steep slopes and streams, obstacles crop up for riders to jump, and twisting paths challenge riders to create bursts of speed along the way. And the whole course is to be completed in less than five minutes!

How does Downhill Fred do it without getting hurt? He stays in control all the time. He keeps his body in top physical shape and constantly works on technical skills like turning and jumping obstacles. What's more, before each race, he practices the course and plans out a riding strategy.

Mountain Biking Tips

RIDE SAFELY Don't go off-roading or hit the trails alone. Always ride with one or more friends and tell an adult where you are going. Mountain bike trails can be dangerous terrain. So practice the following moves and maneuvers before you try them on the trail.

BUNNY HOPS Practice bunny hops, or small jumps, without any obstacles before trying to jump over anything. Ride forward and pull up the handlebars (see above). At the top of the pull, push your hands and body forward and bend your knees. Stay leaning forward to land.

TURNS Brake before you turn and accelerate through the turn (pedal if you can). This will leave your wheels free and help your bike keep solid contact with the ground during the turn.

ROCKY BEDS Stay loose and let your bike flop around as much as possible as you ride over beds of rocks. Keep your weight centered over your bike and try to follow the smoothest path.

MUD Try to turn on the most solid areas. Head for grass whenever possible. Brake sooner and for longer than on dry land. Use the back brake for a more controllable skid. Sit back to keep the weight light on the front wheel.

DROPS 'N' TROUGHS Stay loose to drop (ride off an edge down a steep vertical slope) or ride troughs (drops followed by a steep uphill.) Center your weight over your bike. Pull up the handlebars to clear the top. Then bend your knees to let the back suck up. Try to land on the slope with both wheels at the same time.

"Tour de Tough"

Don't let the name fool you. The Tour de France is no leisurely tour through the French countryside. The world's greatest bicycle race is 21 days of hot, grinding, and grueling cycling through more than 3400 km (2125 mi) of long roads and steep mountains with only two days of rest.

The race is divided into 21 stages. Each stage takes place on a different day and some include sprints or climbing races up mountains. Maybe it should be called the "Tour de Tough"!

Nevertheless, every year 20 or more teams of eight riders each come from all over the world to give it all they've got. The team riders, or *équipiers* in French, try to help the team leader get into the best position to win. How? By staying in front of the leader so he can save energy by drafting (see *Get into the Draft,* page 40).

The *équipiers* also supply spare parts for the leader's bicycle if needed. During the final sprints, the leader breaks away from the *équipiers* and pedals like mad to the finish line. If the leader wins, it's a victory for the entire team. Hurray!

Grease Monkey
ZONE

So you've been popping a few wheelies, racing your heart out, grinding through puddles, and wiping out big time. And your bike, well, it's just not the same cool machine it used to be. Perhaps the frame's caked in mud, or the chain no longer moves smoothly, or the tires are, well, kind of flat. Or perhaps you haven't ridden your bike all winter long. Whatever the case may be, it's time for a tune-up. Get set to enter the Grease Monkey Zone. Prepare to get gunky like a true grease monkey!

Tune-up to Ride

Clean Your Machine

Need a little motivation to get started? Here are three good reasons to clean your bike:

• Dirt, sand, and mud can scratch your bike and jam its moving parts.

• If dirt, sand, or mud sticks on your bike, parts of your bike can break.

• Cleaning your bike regularly can add years to its life!

Check the *Tool Box* opposite and round up what you need. Then follow the steps below for a squeaky-clean machine.

Be careful not to get your fingers or hands stuck in any moving parts, such as the spokes, chain, or chainring. Some of that oily and greasy stuff on your bike should be there. See *Oil It and Grease It*, page 51, to find out where.

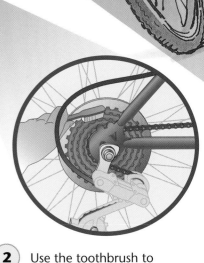

1 Wet the toothbrush and gently clean any dirt off the front and rear derailleurs. (Most bikes have a rear derailleur. Some have both a front and rear derailleur, and some don't have any at all.) Let them dry. Then oil them where shown.

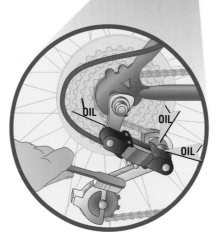

2 Use the toothbrush to clean the teeth on the chainrings and sprockets.

TOOL BOX

water bucket
bike soap or dish soap
old tooth-brush or bike brush
old towel
BICYCLE SOAP
BIKE OIL
old sponge
steel wool
BIKE GREASE
bike oil
bike grease

Can't find some of this stuff at home? Try your local bike shop.

Don't use a hose on your bike, or else water may get into parts of your bike that won't drain!

3 Clean the saddle (a leather saddle needs special leather soap), frame, forks, handlebars, and tires with the sponge and soapy water.

4 Use the toothbrush to clean all the dirt off the front and back brake pads. If any dirt is stuck on hard, scrub it off with the steel wool.

5 Use the towel to clean the front and rear wheel hubs and in between the chainrings and sprockets.

GREASE

GREASE

6 Clean the pedals with the sponge and soapy water. Let the pedals dry. Then grease both ends of each crank where shown.

Fast Fact

Bike or car wax can make your bike shine. Rub it on the frame of your bike with a cloth until the frame glows!

Sky Riding

If the pedals that turned the propeller on the *Daedalus* airplane hadn't been in tip-top mechanical shape, the plane would have crashed into the sea. In 1988, a Greek cycling champ Kanellos Kanellopoulos pedaled the lightweight plane across the sky over the Aegean Sea from the island of Crete to Santorini. The champ pedaled 120 km (74 mi) for 3 hours and 54 minutes straight. And if the pedals had jammed even for a moment, he would have splashed into the drink. Students at the Massachusetts Institute of Technology built the one-seat plane to recreate the mythical flight of *Daedalus*, the hero of the Greek myth *The Minotaur*. But the flight of the *Daedalus* plane was no myth. It set the record for the longest human-powered flight in the world!

Nuts and Bolts

You don't have to be an extreme biker to shake loose the nuts and bolts on your bike. Just regular, everyday riding can loosen them up. And if you don't tighten them back up, they may get bent out of shape. Here's what to do.

TOOL BOX

chain lube

old towel

bike degreaser

bike grease

BIKE OIL

bike oil

Allen key or screwdriver

bike wrench or adjustable wrench

Safety Alert: Handle bike degreaser very carefully. Wear rubber gloves and follow the safety directions that come with it.

50

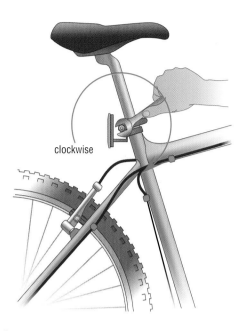

clockwise

1 Use the wrench to tighten ALL the nuts and bolts on your bike as shown.

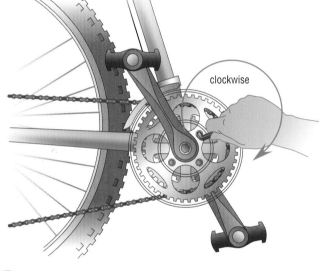

clockwise

2 Use the Allen key, or screwdriver, to tighten the chainring bolts as shown. (Some bikes have rivets, which can't be tightened.)

Coaster Brake Alert: If you pedal backwards to brake, you have a coaster brake. So you can't turn the pedals backwards in step 2 (right) or *Chain* (next page). Turn the pedals forward instead and make sure the back wheel is lifted off the ground so the bike doesn't move.

Oil It and Grease It

Oil and grease aren't just gunky junk. They are lubricants that help the moving parts of your bike slide easily without sticking or scratching. As you ride your bike, the oil and grease ooze out. Rain, puddles, and bike washing also wash them out. So it's a good idea to oil and grease your bike at the beginning, middle, and end of the biking season.

1 Use the towel to clean out old lubricants from the red and yellow circular areas above. Clean the wheel hubs and in between the chainrings and sprockets as shown in step 5 on page 49. Then at the joints between the moving parts, oil the red areas and grease the yellow ones.

backwards

2 Apply chain lube to the chain as you slowly turn the pedals backwards as shown.

Check It Out

IS YOUR BIKE ROAD READY?

Run through this checklist each time you go for a ride. Then you'll spot mechanical trouble before it starts!

Wheels and Gears

• Check your wheels for broken or bent spokes. Check your sprockets and chainrings for any broken teeth. Have a repair shop fix them.

Brakes

Squeeze your brake levers and...

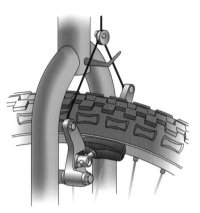

• ...check if the brake pads line up and press firmly against the tire rim as shown. If not, the brake pads may need to be realigned, refit, or replaced. Or the brake cables may need to be replaced. Take your bike to a repair shop to find out.

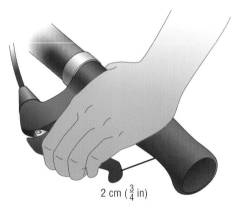

2 cm ($\frac{3}{4}$ in)

• ...check how much room is left between the brake levers and the handlebars. If there's less than shown here, have a repair shop tighten the brake cables or fix the brakes.

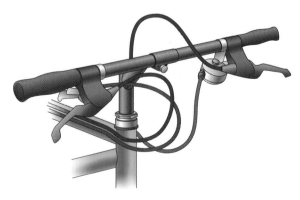

• ...check that the cables are free of knots and kinks as shown. If not, straighten them out.

Tires

40 psi (2.8 bar)

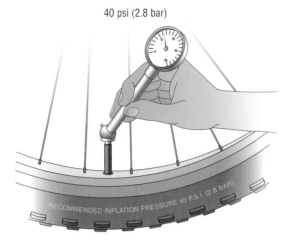

- Check the tire treads for trapped bits and stones. Protect your eyes. Carefully remove any bits with a screwdriver, so they don't pierce your tires.

- Check the tire pressure with a pressure gauge as shown. Make sure it matches the recommended pressure on the side of the tire.

Chain

- If the pressure is too low, the tire may puncture easily. Pump air into the tire as shown. Follow the directions on the bike pump, and use the pressure gauge to check that the tire reaches the recommended pressure.

- Check that the chain moves smoothly as shown. If it gets stuck, scrub it with a sponge and soapy water. Scrape off stubborn dirt with an old toothbrush. Remove old oil and grime with bike degreaser.

- If the tire pressure is too high, the tire may burst. Let some air out as shown.

- Dry the chain well with an old rag, or else it may rust and foul up. Then oil it with special chain lube as shown.

Replacing the Chain

Sooner or later your chain is bound to fall off. It's just a fact of life, er, bikes! And it often happens in the middle of nowhere, when you can't get any help. Here's how to troubleshoot your way out of this sticky situation.

NO Bike Repair SHOPS for 80 km (50 mi)

(2) Pick up the chain with a rag, paper towel, or handful of leaves to keep your hands clean.

(3) Check if the chain is broken or bent. If so, don't put it back on your bike, because a damaged chain can break your gear system. Walk your bike to a repair shop.

(4) If the chain isn't broken or bent, you're in luck. Clean off as much dirt as possible. Protect your eyes. Then remove any rocks or bits stuck in it with a stick, screwdriver, or pocket knife.

(1) As soon as the chain falls off, stop pedaling and get off your bike. Otherwise, the chain may bend or break.

5 If the chain has fallen off a rear sprocket, hook it onto the top teeth of any rear sprocket.

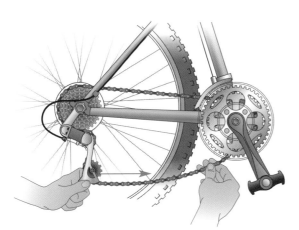

6 If the chain has fallen off a chainring and your bike has a rear derailleur tension lever as shown, push the lever forward to give the chain some slack. Then hook the chain onto the chainring.

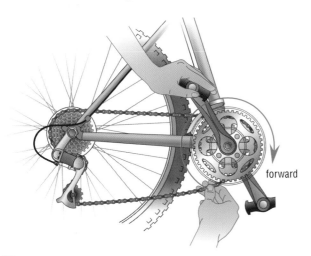

forward

7 Slowly turn the crank forward and guide the chain over the chainring as shown.

Dinosaurs Are an Oily Bunch

Did you know chain lube comes from dinosaurs? No kidding! It's made of oil found deep in the ground. Scientists don't know exactly how the oil formed, but many think it's left over from the age of the dinosaurs. They think that when the dinosaurs died out, many other creatures on the land and in the sea died, too. Then the dinosaurs, plants, and other creatures were buried in layers of mud and rock. Over millions of years, these layers were covered and pushed around by earthquakes and erupting volcanoes. The trapped remains of the dinosaurs and creatures decomposed, or broke down, into oil. So when you oil your chain, you may be recycling a T-Rex!

8 Ride your bike slowly to make sure that the chain is in place. If your bike feels weird or the chain gets stuck, stop and check the chain. Is it in the correct place? Remove any stones or twigs stuck in it and try riding again. If your bike still feels strange, walk it to a repair shop.

That's Radical

Bikes at Work

Have bikes got a job to do? You bet! Over the years, bikes have delivered police, firefighters, emergency medics, soldiers, and couriers to the scene on time.

In the early 1900s, bikes were faster and more reliable than cars. So firefighters equipped bicycles with a hose, siren, flashlight, and crowbar to speed to fires. Back then, soldiers also rode bikes on the job. Soldiers' bikes held a rifle and folded up in half. That way soldiers could carry their bikes over their shoulders if the terrain got too tough for pedaling.

Nowadays, delivery couriers and police ride bikes to cut through heavy city traffic in record time. "Cops on bikes" patrol units are becoming popular because riding bikes helps police stay close to communities. It's much easier to stop and chat with people on a bike than from a car!

Riding bikes also helps police get to hard-to-reach places where many crimes happen and cars can't go. In fact, cops go to training school to learn how to ride bikes down staircases.

Gear Up
FOR THE ROAD

Hey you! Yeah *you!* Ride safely and "be seen on the scene" when you hit the road with your two-wheel machine. Bone up on the Rules of the Road and wear bright clothes. Put reflectors on yourself and your bike. And remember this: you're not the only one on the road or trail. Far from it. That's why the Rules of the Road are definitely not made to be broken. Watch out for other cyclists, cars, and traffic. And don't ever forget the number one rule—have fun!

RIDE THIS WAY

Cool Gear

Y ou don't need loads of gear to take your bike for a spin. But here's how gearing up for safety and comfort can help you get the most out of your ride.

Lock

Everybody knows bikes are a hot-ticket item. Unfortunately, if you leave yours unattended without locking it up, it may not be waiting for you when you get back! Make sure you loop the lock around and through the bike frame. Try to lock the wheels also.

Bell

Brrrrring! A funky bell can help you warn other traffic you're coming their way.

Reflector

No bike or rider should be without reflectors. These shiny, plastic disks or tape reflect light, so you and your bike can be easily seen day or night.

Dynamo light

Mount this light on your bike and light your way with your own pedal power. No kidding! The wheel of a dynamo light presses against one of your tires. And as you pedal, the tire turns and pushes the dynamo wheel. This generates electricity. In fact, the faster you pedal, the brighter the bulb glows!

Water bottle

Bring a water bottle on long rides to quench your thirst.

Helmet

Don't ride without one! Bike helmets are designed to protect your head from hard knocks. No wonder helmets are called brain buckets. Certified bicycle helmets are crash-tested to make sure they're up to snuff. First, the helmet is strapped onto a dummy head and dropped onto a metal floor. Sensors measure the force when the helmet hits the floor. The helmet is then certified only if the force is small enough not to "kill" the dummy or rattle its "brains."

Sunglasses

If you think cyclists wear shades just to look cool, think again! Sunglasses protect your eyes from flying dirt, bugs, wind, and the sun's harmful ultraviolet rays.

Biker clothes

Biker tops and shorts are often made of bright reflective colors, so you can be easily seen day or night. And they fit snugly. That way they don't flap in the wind, which slows you down, or rub against your body, which may irritate your skin. Cyclists wear lots of layers on long treks. Then they can add or remove layers as the temperature changes throughout the day.

Here's how a bike helmet protects your noggin.

- A foamlike inner lining works the same way as the gloves boxers wear to protect their hands. When the helmet is hit hard, the lining squishes to absorb the force of impact. But unlike a boxing glove, it doesn't return to its original shape afterward. So once your helmet takes a hard hit, you should replace it.
- A hard outer shell helps absorb impacts and lessen their force by spreading them out over a large area. It also protects the inner lining from water and dirt.
- Straps and buckles are specially designed to keep the helmet securely on your head during an impact. See the instructions that come with your helmet to find out exactly how to adjust them.
- Vents let body heat out and air in to help keep you cool. But you won't find air vents on most mountain bike helmets. Otherwise, branches and rocks might get in!

Rules of the Road

Follow these rules and tips to ride safely.

1. Always wear a helmet when you ride. It's the law in many places.

2. Avoid riding on the road whenever possible. Ride on bike paths or trails.

3. If you must ride on the road, stay as far to the right-hand side as possible. Follow all traffic rules, such as stopping at red lights and stop signs.

4. Always ride in the same direction as cars. Ride in as straight a line as possible. Don't zigzag or swerve around parked cars.

5. Before you ride out onto a street, stop and look both ways. Wait until all cars have passed.

6. Making left turns on the road is dangerous, because cars approaching from both directions can collide with you. So to turn left at an intersection, dismount and walk your bike across the crosswalks instead.

7. Be alert when you ride past parked cars. Keep about one metre (3 ft) away from the cars. Watch for car mirrors, opening doors, and cars pulling out of parking spots.

8. Before you make a turn, always check over your shoulder for oncoming cars. Use hand signals to let drivers know what you plan to do:

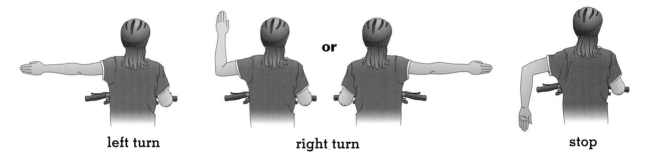

left turn   **right turn**   **stop**

9. If you ride at night, make sure you have front and rear lights and reflectors on you and your bike. Wear light-colored clothes.

10. Try to avoid any holes in the road, rocks, sewer grates, or puddles, so your bike doesn't get stuck.

Check It Out

YOU'RE THE DRIVER

Just how tough is it for drivers to see cyclists on the road? Try this experiment and see. Ask an adult to park a car in a driveway, or another spot away from traffic, and then help you with this activity.

• Sit in the driver's seat. You may need to sit on an old phone book or pillows to see out the windshield, rear and side view mirrors. But don't worry if you can't reach the gas pedal—you aren't going anywhere!

• Ask the adult to adjust the rear and side view mirrors for you as if you were a driver.

• Have the adult or a friend ride a bike toward the car from behind and pass it on the right. Pretend you are driving. Look forward through the windshield and take brief glimpses at the rear and side view mirrors.

• Did you see the cyclist ride by?

• Have the cyclist ride past again, but this time on the left-hand side. And whatever you do, don't open your car door!

• Did you see the cyclist ride by this time? When did you first notice the cyclist? What if your attention was divided by concentrating on driving the car, keeping track of other cars and trucks, talking to passengers, and listening to the radio at the same time? Can you see why it's tough for drivers to see cyclists?

Glossary

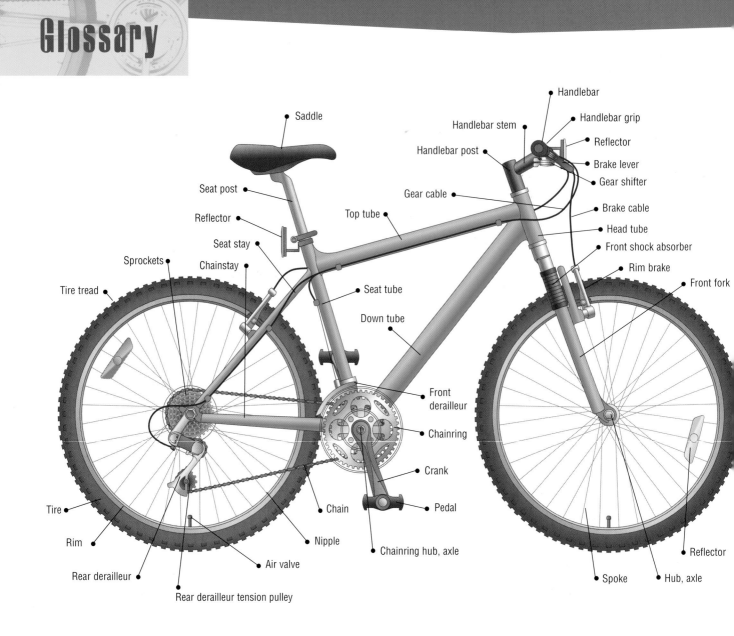

Saddle

Handlebar

Handlebar stem

Handlebar grip

Handlebar post

Reflector

Seat post

Gear cable

Brake lever

Gear shifter

Reflector

Top tube

Brake cable

Seat stay

Head tube

Sprockets

Chainstay

Front shock absorber

Tire tread

Seat tube

Rim brake

Front fork

Down tube

Tire

Front derailleur

Chainring

Crank

Pedal

Rim

Chain

Rear derailleur

Nipple

Chainring hub, axle

Air valve

Reflector

Spoke

Hub, axle

Rear derailleur tension pulley

adjustable wrench: tool for loosening and tightening nuts and bolts of different sizes

aerodynamic: designed to move with minimal air resistance

air resistance: force of air against an object's movement

Allen key: six-sided tool for adjusting screws

banked turn: sloped track at a curve

bicycle: vehicle that has two (bi) wheels (cycle)

bike degreaser: solvent, found in bike shops, that dissolves and removes grease

bike wrench: tool made for adjusting bike nuts and bolts

BMX: bicycle motocross

bolt: metal rod with a head used for holding parts together

cadence: speed of pedaling, measured in revolutions (or strokes) per minute

centripetal force: the force that acts on an object to keep it in circular motion

chain lube: special oil used for lubricating bike chains

chainring: front toothed wheel that the chain loops onto, sometimes called front sprocket or chainwheel

coaster brake: brake in the hub of the wheel, activated by pedaling backwards

derailleur: gear shifting mechanism that moves the chain on and off the chainrings and rear wheel sprockets

downhill mountain racing: bike racing that goes only downhill and over obstacles

drafting: riding behind another cyclist for aerodynamic advantage

drop: a racing obstacle—riding off an edge and down a near-vertical slope

équipiers: members of a bike racing team

fairing: outer structure of a moving object used to reduce air resistance

fishtail: skid in which the back end of the bike skids out of control in a zigzag

forks: frame tubes that hold the wheels

frame size: bicycle size: distance from the chainring axle to the top of the seat tube

freestyle: creative trick riding

gear: toothed wheel that fits onto another toothed wheel or chain to transmit motion

gear ratio: number of times the sprocket turns the rear wheel for each pedal turn

gear system: one or more gears that work together

grease: thick oily lubricant

height: distance from the top of the seat tube to the ground

high wheeler: bike from the 1800s with a large front wheel and small back wheel

hub: central part of a wheel

inner tube: balloonlike rubber container in a tire that holds air

lubricant: oil or grease used to reduce friction between moving parts of a bike

mechanism: parts that work together to make something move

moto: BMX race or heat in a BMX race

motocross: motorcycle race in tough terrain—sharp curves and steep hills

nipple: adjustable nut on the wheel rim used to hold and tighten the spokes

nut: small piece of metal with a threaded hole in it that's used to secure a bolt

pressure gauge: device used to measure pressure

recumbent: bicycle that is ridden in a reclined position

rim brake: hand-operated brake that forces pads to press against the wheel rim, sometimes called caliper brake

safety bicycle: the first bike with one gear, and front and back wheels the same size

sprint: short ride at full speed

stroke: one full pedal revolution

suspension system: springs, dampers, or the like that reduce shocks from bumps

tandem: bicycle built for two or more riders

terrain: area of ground

time trial: individual, non-team race against the clock over a certain distance

Tour de France: bike race around France

tread: thick protective outer layer of a tire

trial: any kind of cycling test, stunt, or race

triathlon: three-sport race made up of biking, swimming, and running

trough: drop followed by a steep uphill

unrideable bicycle: bike built to fall over

velodrome: banked bicycle racing track

wheelie: riding on the rear wheel with the front wheel off the ground